LUFTWAFFE AT WAR

German Bombers Over Russia

A close-up of the nose of a Ju 88A-5 showing clearly the cockpit with the pilot and his observer sitting on his right. Centre left is the gondola with the bombsight which is protected by thick armoured glass. Later, many A-positions in these bombers were rebuilt and fitted with a cable device. Other aircraft were modified to take an MG FF above the bombsight for low-level attacks.

LUFTWAFFE AT WAR

German Bombers Over Russia

Manfred Griehl

Greenhill Books
LONDON

Stackpole Books
PENNSYLVANIA

Greenhill Books

German Bombers over Russia first published 2000 by
Greenhill Books, Lionel Leventhal Limited, Park
House, 1 Russell Gardens, London NW11 9NN
www.greenhillbooks.com
and
Stackpole Books, 5067 Ritter Road, Mechanicsburg,
PA 17055, USA

British Library Cataloguing in Publication Data
Griehl, Manfred
German Bombers over Russia. – (Luftwaffe at war)
1.Germany. Luftwaffe – History   2.World War,
1939–1945 – Aerial operations, German   3. World
War, 1939–1945 – Campaigns – Russia (Federation)
I. Title
940.5'44943

ISBN   1-85367-423-0

*Library of Congress Cataloging-in-Publication Data
available*

Designed by DAG Publications Ltd
Design by David Gibbons
Layout by Anthony A. Evans
Printed in Singapore

GERMAN BOMBERS OVER RUSSIA

The first flush of an overwhelming tactical success for the *Luftwaffe* bomber forces happened with the defeat of Poland. Furthermore the campaigns in Denmark and Norway ended with complete victory for the *Wehrmacht*. With the fall of France it seemed that German military power would be strong enough to become victorious all over Europe. However British air defence forces resisted the German raids to bring about the first major failure of German air power. Hitler's continental policy, the invasion of the Balkans and the capture of Crete, accompanied by the establishment of the *Luftwaffe* in Italy, the anti-shipping raids and the Battle of the Atlantic, were responsible for many operational losses which weakened the strength of the bomber *Gruppen* of the *Kampfgeschwader*. But the *Luftwaffe*'s most dangerous campaign followed in summer 1941: the invasion of the Soviet Union with whom Germany had shared a non-aggression pact.

For many years Adolf Hitler had thought about plans to attack Russia in a huge combined operation. The early preparations for the new campaign had been underway since October 1940 under the top secret designation *Ostbauprogramm* (Eastern Construction Programme). In the newly occupied Polish territories several ground units of the *Luftwaffe* and other formations started to establish an impressive infrastructure for several *Luftwaffe* flying units. That meant the construction of new airfields and depots. In April and May 1941 the first fighter and bomber formations left the other war theatres and within a few weeks became available for the impending operations against the Soviet Union. At the opening of the Russian campaign in June 1941 three *Luftflotten* (1, 2 and 4) were ranged on the Russian Front. In the northern part of the Front, parts of the *Luftflotte* 5 were deployed in Norway and were assisted by Finnish flyers. Additionally the allied air forces of Hungary, Romania and Italy with smaller contingents immediately entered the new war theatre.

The sector of *Luftflotte* 1 looked towards Leningrad and included all three Baltic countries. That of *Luftflotte* 2 comprised the central part of the Front and initially headed to Minsk and Smolensk. Finally *Luftflotte* 4, which had been withdrawn from the Balkans, was responsible for the southern sector of the Front which had a total length of more than 900 miles. The *Luftwaffe* forces along the Eastern Front comprised no less than some 2770 aircraft out of the total *Luftwaffe* first-line strength of 4300 and consisted of 775 long-range Do 17, He 111 and Ju 88 bombers, some 300 dive-bombers and more than 900 single-seat Bf 109 fighters and two-seat Bf 110 *Zerstören*.

As in previous campaigns, an initial very heavy blow was struck at the opposing air force. The Red Air Force was concentrating in larger numbers, itself preparing for an offensive after it had become clear to Stalin and his supreme staff that a German attack on Russia was imminent because so many units of the *Wehrmacht* and the *Luftwaffe* had been moved to Poland, East Prussia, Romania and Hungary. The surprise attacks at the start of the offensive inflicted heavy losses on Russian aircraft on the ground. The main thrust developed on the central part of the Front where the forces of the II and VIII *Fliegerkorps* were subordinated under the command of *Luftflotte* 2. In addition, day fighters and other aircraft were fitted to drop small SD 1 and SD 2 bombs from bomblet dispensers and engaged in low-level attacks on enemy installations everywhere. So-called 'butterfly bombs', the SDs were carried in 1 kg or 2 kg dispensers which, when dropped, opened in mid air and scattered the bombs over a wide area. SD bombs were at their most effective when used against troop concentrations. Also, mine layers tried to paralyse the Soviet Union's sea communications and isolate the heavy units of the Red Navy.

The rapid advance of the German *Wehrmacht* into Russia caused many casualties and weakened the *Luftwaffe* bomber forces too. The bomber *Gruppen*, such as the KG 51 *'Edelweiss'*, lost half of its crews during the initial combat missions. In the middle of July 1941 the Battle of Smolensk began. Several Soviet armies were hit by the *Luftwaffe* bombers and lost major parts of their operational strength. The German units continued eastwards. It became possible for them to establish new front line bases in Russia, thus enabling the *Luftwaffe* to make bombing raids on the Russian capital, Moscow, on 21 July and 22 July, mainly with He 111H bombers.

By the end of July 1941, due to the vast size of the advancing fronts, the German bomber forces had insufficient strength to fulfil all operational duties. In order to meet local tactical requirements the main effort switched from Army Group Centre opposite Moscow to Army Group North opposite Leningrad. One result of this was the transfer in August 1941 of command of the VIII *Fliegerkorps* (mainly a dive-bombing force) from *Luftflotte* 2 to *Luftflotte* 1. More than 400 close-support aircraft of the *Luftwaffe* were soon concentrated there. During that month the central sector (Army Group Centre) stayed static while Army Group South tried to occupy the Ukraine with the help of *Luftflotte* 4. The main fighting was at the Black Sea and the harbour of Odessa. While armoured forces advanced to Gomel the resistance of the Red Army became stronger. German resources were not strong enough to hit all necessary targets to enable the fast movement of the armoured troops.

In October 1941 Leningrad was encircled by Army Group North and the city was subsequently attacked by German bombers. Army Group South encircled large numbers of the Red Army but, following the victory at Kiev in September, the main focus of the *Wehrmacht* again switched to Army Group Centre and Moscow. More than 600 heavy bombers were brought together to hit the capital during a limited number of air raids following the ground offensive in October 1941. It was suggested that Moscow should be encircled from the north but due to the Russian resistance there was no chance to fulfil Hitler's demands.

In November 1941 airfield conditions all over Russia worsened because of mud and snow. Additionally, over the southern part of the Eastern Front, the Red Air Force was able to prevent a Germany victory in the air. Despite many close-support missions and several level bombing raids carried out by the *Kampfgeschwader* German operations were severely curtailed during the winter campaign of 1941/42. The failure of the attack on Moscow and heavy raids of the He 111 bombers on targets in the centre of the capital brought about severe losses due to well-organised Russian anti-aircraft defences and the many Russian fighters that had been held back to defend the capital. During the severe winter German air strength was reduced to some 1700 aircraft, insufficient to carry out all of the necessary offensive operations on the Eastern Front.

Between January and June 1942 the *Luftwaffe* bombers were needed to stop the Russian advance heading for Kharkov and Smolensk via new formations of the Red Army sent from territories east of the Urals. After the operations in the Moscow region failed, the *Luftwaffe* bomber units were concentrated to assist the *Wehrmacht* which was now reorganised for a new powerful campaign with the maximum possible forces along the southern sector of the front (Army Group South). The new target was the oilfields of the Caucasus. The first step was to cover the German southern flank by the complete occupation of the Crimea and to destroy Russian forces at the Kerch Peninsula. With the help of some 600 warplanes subordinated to the command of *Luftflotte* 4 a major assault on Sevastopol was initiated, including many bombing raids by the *Kampfgeschwader*. Also transport formations flying the He 111 were engaged in laying sea mines in the main Black Sea shipping routes.

The main offensive opened in the first week of July 1942 with operations by the VIII *Fliegerkorps* against Voronezh. Subsequently the operations zone was extended southwards while armoured formations of the *Wehrmacht* moved steadily forwards. The Germans advanced rapidly to the line of the River Don and occupied the western part of the Caucasus. Simultaneously, bombing raids were carried out to hit the Russian lines of communication. Because there was a lack of heavy bombers the *Luftwaffe* failed to destroy the major reserves of the Red Army and to eliminate the industrial centres far behind the Urals that were supplying the Soviet forces. Most of the German bombers were needed for close air support, to attack the major ports along the Caucasus coast and to mine the Volga. But due to the low number of serviceable bombers only a few raids achieved any level of success.

The German air policy during late summer 1942 was dominated by the inability of the German High Command to decide on the next step. Because it was not possible to cover two major battlefields, Stalingrad and the Volga, and the Caucasus, the *Luftwaffe* was forced to split its forces. A very high level of effort was maintained at the city of Stalingrad by the VIII *Fliegerkorps* operating under *Luftflotte* 4. It was here that most of the German dive-bombers were concentrated.

The number of raids and severe losses caused by fighter aircraft of the Red Air Force were responsible for many *Luftwaffe* bomber units being withdrawn from the southern part of the Eastern Front to be re-equipped with new crews and aircraft. Besides Stalingrad, the *Luftwaffe* bomber formations had to attack separately the besieged city of Leningrad as well as the capital, Moscow. Although strong formations from the Leningrad front were sent to the Stalingrad region, the Red Army continued to defend the ruins of the city.

Meanwhile the lines of supply were extended to secure a large-scale and long-term *Luftwaffe* operation against the region of Stalingrad.

Finally, at the end of October 1942, the Red Army had gathered forces strong enough to begin a counter-offensive at a time when the *Luftwaffe* was forced to defend the *Wehrmacht*'s 300 km front with less than 100 combat aircraft. The reason for the depleted air strength was the withdrawal of bomber forces to the coasts of the Mediterranean Sea where Allied offensives were responsible for the loss of German positions in Libya and Tunisia. The operational strength of the I and VIII *Fliegerkorps* in southern Russia was reduced from a total of 1050 combat aircraft to less than 700. After some 400 *Luftwaffe* aircraft had been sent to the Mediterranean the remaining German forces were unable to defend the Caucasus area. The encircled 6th Army at Stalingrad and the weakened 17th Army at the Kuban bridgehead (across from the Crimea) lost their defence capabilities due to a lack of air cover by the *Luftwaffe*. Many of the *Luftwaffe* bombers were used to transport necessary supplies to isolated German forces in Russia. Besides many Ju 52/3m transport aircraft, all kind of bombers, especially He 111Hs but also He 177As and Fw 200Cs, were engaged in air transport missions. Russian day fighters and AA batteries caused heavy losses over Stalingrad.

After expending major resources the *Wehrmacht* was forced to give up its front line positions. The Red Army recaptured Voronezh late in January 1943 and by mid-February was heading for Rostov and Kharkov. The Kuban bridgehead in the Kuban Peninsula was threatened by strong Russian forces. It proceeded to sweep forward to the mouth of the Don at Rostov. The number of serviceable German bombers dropped lower and lower while Soviet air power grew steadily with the help of the Western Allies. On 16 February 1943 the city of Kharkov passed back into Russian hands and a few days later Belgorod was lost. Due to low numbers of German aircraft only local successes could be achieved. *Störkampfstaffeln* (ad hoc ground-attack units equipped with second-line, often antiquated, aircraft types armed with small bombs) and *Nachtschlachtgruppen* (similar units used for night operations) were established as auxiliary units to attack the enemy's lines of communication. Only a limited number of German bombers, mostly Ju 88A-4s and He

111H-6s, were available to destroy targets behind the front line. Between 21 February and the end of March 1943 a German counter-offensive resulted in the recapture of Kharkov. Compared with only 350 sorties flown earlier in the year, for a short period it was possible to fly some 1200 missions. Additionally special *Staffeln* (9/KG 3, 14/KG 27 and 9/KG 55) were engaged in attacking the Russian railway system. In April 1943 the *Wehrmacht* became active on the Kuban Peninsula but suffered heavy losses because the *Luftwaffe* was unable to secure local air superiority.

From the beginning of May 1943 the *Luftwaffe* concentration in the Crimea was reduced in order to attack the Kursk region where a huge counter-offensive was being prepared by the *Wehrmacht*. Some 2500 aircraft were tasked to support the Panzer divisions on the front line battlefields in June 1943. Furthermore the local Soviet airfields were bombed by the *Luftwaffe* and heavy raids against industrial targets were undertaken to weaken the Red Army. But again the weak *Luftwaffe* forces were unable to secure air superiority and suffered heavy losses. On 22 July 1943 the German ground forces retreated under the pressure of Soviet tank divisions. Early in August 1943 Orel and Belgorod were recaptured by Soviet forces. The way was now open for powerful Russian offensives. Between August and December 1943 the Russian offensive towards the Dnieper drove the Germans back. After the reverse at Kursk the He 111 bomber forces tried to defend the Donets region despite the numerical inferiority of their own *Kampfgeschwader*. Because the operational strength of most bomber units was limited during winter 1943/44 their own capacity for attacking targets far away from the front was very poor and therefore they did not succeed in mounting offensive operations as suggested by *Generaloberst* Korten. Because there was a lack of heavy bombers, especially He 177As, many important Soviet industries could produce tanks and weapons on a large scale without being interrupted by enemy air raids.

With the Russian re-occupation of the Crimea and the spring offensive the *Wehrmacht* was forced to mount a new defensive operation in northern Romania. Also, Hungary was threatened by overwhelming enemy forces preparing for an advance into Germany.

On 10 June 1944 the main Soviet offensive opened with a major assault on the Finnish frontier. On 23 June 1944, a huge Soviet offensive attacked *Heeresgruppe Mitte* (Army Group Centre). By 3 July 1944 Vitebsk, Mogilev and Minsk had fallen to the advancing Russians. Because several fighter units had been sent to Germany and to Western Europe to take part in the defence of the West following D-Day and the Normandy breakout, the protection of the bombers operating on the Eastern Front was significantly reduced. There were only some thirty bombers available to *Luftflotte* 4 and some 300 in *Luftflotte* 6 (which had taken over command of the central sector following *Luftflotte* 2's move to the Mediterranean), while no bombers were available to *Luftflotte* 1.

Under pressure from the Red Army many German positions were lost and the *Kampfgeschwader* had to be withdrawn to Poland. In mid-September the eastern and south-eastern fronts became fused into one as the Russians squeezed the German forces into a narrower front having now reached the borders of Yugoslavia. Romania terminated the alliance with the *Deutsches Reich* and joined the Allies on 23 August 1944. Finland departed on 4 September 1944. The limited number of German bomber units, handicapped by lack of fuel and spare parts, was unable to carry out major operations along the Eastern Front. The Russian bomber forces increased to considerable numbers of mostly twin-engined bombers while the *Luftwaffe* could operate only some eighty bombers over the Eastern Front.

Early in January 1945 Warsaw, Lodz, Cracow, along with Allenstein and Insterburg in East Prussia, were captured by the Russians. After the failure of a German counter-offensive in Hungary the last bombers were used for transport duties and a limited number of raids were aimed at bridges captured by the Red Army in the east. Only a few crews survived these dangerous missions to return to Germany. During the final battles only a very few German bombers were engaged. The air attack against Russia had ultimately failed.

Two Ju 88A-5s on an airfield in Northern Poland, warming up for an attack on enemy targets in the USSR.

Left: Two He 111H-11s of *Gruppenstab* of the II *Gruppe* of *Kampfgeschwader* 53 'Legion Condor' returning without bombs from their target in Russia. The aircraft are painted in a standard camouflage scheme (70/71/65) and feature a yellow band around the rear section of the fuselage.

Above: One He 111H-6 of KG 27 moving out of its cover between the trees of a small forest in the east. The aircraft is armed with a heavy MG FF in the nose to destroy lightly armoured enemy vehicles moving up to the battlefield. The aircraft is probably loaded with eight bombs inside the bomb-bay.

Above: Four aircrew of I/KG 27 posing in front of an He 111H in Russia during the first part of the campaign. Two crew members wear the summer-weight flying overall and flying helmets made from leather. One of the others wears a cuff title bearing *Kampfgeschwader* 'Boelke'.

Left: An officer of KG 27 prepares himself for the next briefing. The tip of the tail cone was removed from some bombers and a rearward-firing machine-gun (or grenade launcher) installed. This aircraft is painted in splinter camouflage of 70/71 tones with undersurfaces in blue 65.

Opposite page: During the initial phase of the air war over Russia the German *Kampfgeschwader* were strong enough to attack their targets in large numbers, often assisted by fighters, mostly Bf 109Es and Fs. Later the number of serviceable bombers was severely reduced while the number of Russian fighters steadily grew.

A limited number of He 177A-1s were sent to the Stalingrad area to assist the German ground troops in the encircled city by delivering supply containers with food and ammunition. However, suffered engine and equipment failure, the I/*Fernkampfgruppe* 50 lost several crews in action and was withdrawn.

During autumn and winter it was difficult for the 'black men' (the ground crew, so-called because of the colour of their standard overalls) to maintain and refuel their aircraft without the protection of a hangar. Because of the difficult conditions of the Russian winter it took the men a long time to warm-up the engines of the Ju 88As and He 111Hs each morning and to remove the snow that had fallen in the night.

During the final phase of the Russian campaign some Ju 188s were introduced to increase the reconnaissance capacity of the *Luftwaffe*. Because these aircraft had increased defensive armament they were far more likely to survive a reconnaissance mission than a Ju 88D-1. Here, one of the BMW 801 MA engines is being overhauled.

Right: *Kampfgruppe* 100 operated the He 111H-3 during the initial phase of the Russian campaign. The aircraft being serviced belongs to 1 *Staffel* of the *Gruppe,* which comprised three *Staffeln* each of twelve aircraft. These are equipped with a special wireless operation system, enabling long-range pathfinder missions to be made by day or night. The ground crew has just cleaned the upper surfaces of the twin-engined bomber for the initial attack.

Below: This He 111H-3, operated by *Kampfgeschwader* (KG) 54, is being prepared for further operations under field conditions in summer 1941. The code G1+CH indicates that the bomber is the third aircraft of 1/KG 55. The yellow band painted around the rear part of the fuselage shows that the aircraft is involved in operations over Russia. In the foreground are several general-purpose (GP) bombs for the next mission, having been delivered by Ju 52/3m transport aircraft (background, left).

Above: Belonging to 3 *Staffel* of KG 55, this He 111H-3 is ready for take-off from a front line airfield in Russia. The G1+ML could be armed with up to six MG 15 movable machine-guns for self protection against enemy fighter attacks. During the first phase of the air war over Russia, several German day fighter formations equipped with Bf 109Es and Fs created sufficient air protection.

Below: Because it was impossible for the early He 111H-1s and H-2s to carry heavy bombs longer than the SC 250, due to the vertical-slotted arrangement of the bomb-bay, the H-3 and H-4 and most of the later versions were equipped with PVC 1006 or ETC 2000 bomb racks. The He 111H-6 (5J+IP) shown here fulfilled the demands of the *Kampfgeschwader* because it could carry two large bombs outside the fuselage or one load outside and one inside. The aircraft pictured here is operated by 6/KG 3 '*Blitz*'.

Right: For the 'black men' the arming of bomber aircraft involved a number of difficult duties. Here several men and NCOs are needed to position the SC 250 GP bombs, fitted with 'screechers' or 'Pipes of Jericho' – attachments that made loud, whistling noises as the bombs fell – into the vertical-slotted bomb-bay of this He 111H-6 which belongs to I/KG 26. The purpose of the 'screecher' was to demoralise the enemy. The 1H+HL shown here was later damaged by Russian fighters.

Below: The frontal armament fitted in the glazed cockpit of the He 111H of the III/KG 53 at first comprised only the MG 15 machine-gun but an MG FF (20 mm cannon) was later installed to increase firepower. The small opening between the upper and lower glazed canopy was used for shooting signal flares. The exhaust collector on each side of the Jumo 211D indicates that this bomber belongs to the third II series.

Above: Heavy bombs such as the SC 1000 were often fitted on sleds so that they could be towed by small captured tanks on some of the poorly constructed airfields in Russia. The GP bomb weighed 1000 kg of which 850 kg was explosive. It was 2.8 m in length and 0.65 m in diameter. This and other heavy payloads were loaded under the main fuselage section of the He 111 with the help of a block and tackle and several ground crew.

Below: This Soviet tractor was captured by soldiers of KG 27 on a Russian airfield when the *Kampfgruppen* were moved forward to new bases. The tractor is being used to pull a device behind it to smooth the surface on airfields without runways.

Right: A view inside an early He 111H-2 (1G1+BL) operated by KG 27. The H-2s were later replaced by H-4s and H-6s. On each side of the interior are four vertical ESAC 250/IX bomb slots for SC 250s. In the foreground is the huge main spar that crosses the central part of the fuselage. In the glass house (the cockpit), the pilot's seat is on the left side.

Opposite page, top: The crew of this He 111H-3 of I *Gruppe* f KG 55 were forced to divert their flight to a more eastern airfield after developing problems with the wireless system. The event has drawn the attention of some *Wehrmacht* soldiers. The paint on the leading edges of many of the propeller blades has been worn away during the previous missions. The upper surfaces of the aircraft are painted in shades of dark-green (officially known as 70/71 tones) while the undersurfaces are painted light blue-grey (65 tone). Some of the camouflage paint has also disappeared due to wear and tear.

Opposite page, bottom: Besides the bomber formations of the *Kampfgeschwader* several other units were equipped with the He 111H and P. For example, the *Schleppgruppen*, which towed supply gliders to front line bases and besieged *Wehrmacht* units and were sometimes used for offensive operations. This He 111H belongs to 1/*Schleppgruppe* 4. It crashed in summer 1943 after an engine failure.

Above: One of the ground crew sits on a SC 500 GP bomb with another man who appears to be a *Waffenmeister* (armourer). Around them are several other types of bomb including the SC 250, SC 50 and a few older versions of the SC 500. Behind them is an He 111H-6 used for night raids over Russia, part of 2/KG 27 as indicated by the code 1G+IK.

Opposite page, top: This He 111H-4, equipped with an SC 500, was photographed mid-1942. It was operated by crews of 1/KG 55. The unit came under the command of *Luftflotte* 1 and was based at Tivorograd airfield. Later the unit joined other forces that were ordered to attack enemy targets in the industrial areas of Stalingrad and along the Volga.

Opposite page, bottom: One of the He 111H-3s of III *Gruppe* of KG 27 'Boelke' during a transfer to a front line airbase. In 1942 this *Kampfgruppe* was based in southern Russia and assisted the offensive in the Caucasus as part of the IV *Fliegerkorps* which was subordinated to *Luftflotte* 4. The unit remained in southern Russia and continued its operational career after II *Gruppe* was sent to Langenhagen, Germany, to re-equip.

Right: Seven of the ground crew prepare an SC 1000 GP bomb on a trolley before moving it under a Ju 88A-4's bomb rack. This is a newer version of the SC 1000 with a redesigned fin unit. Two of the 'black men' are working on the three fuses fitted in the body of the SC 1000.

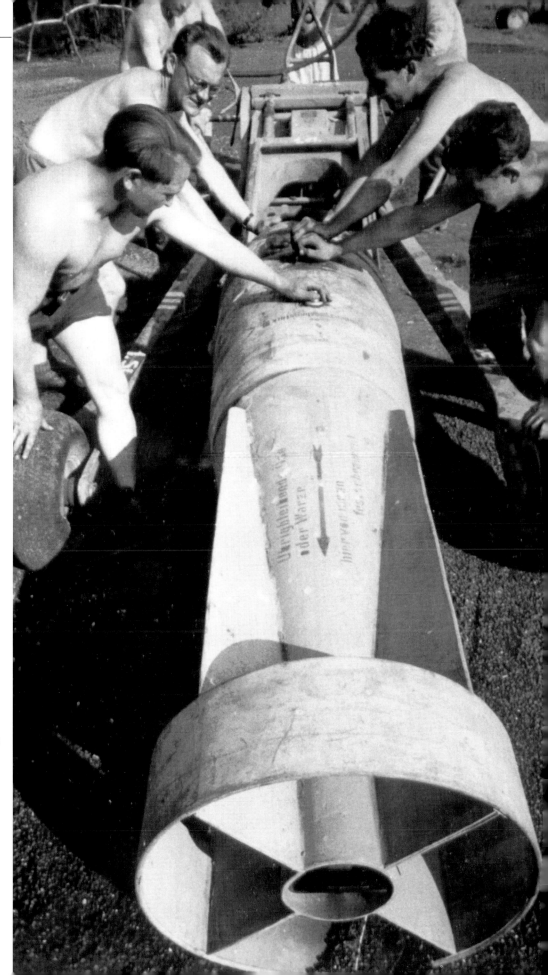

Above: This aircraft, F1+BK, belongs to 1 *Staffel* of *Kampfgeschwader* 77. It has just been loaded with heavy bombs fitted to the external bomb racks under the inner wing sections. The *Kompaniefeldwebel* (Senior Company NCO), in charge of all junior NCOs and other ranks, and more commonly known as *Spiess*, stands with his back to the camera, hands on hips; he can be recognised by the silver rings on his cuffs.

eft: One of the few Ju 88A-6s, special subvariants of the Ju
8 with a large balloon-fender fitted to the nose and wings.
 was too unwieldy to be a success, so the fenders were
moved and the few A-6s that had been built were handed
ver to normal bomber units. They remained recognisable by
e small fairings which had previously been used to attach
e fender to the nose (seen above the tip of the propeller
ade). In front of the A-position (front gun position) of the
ockpit, part of an MG 15 can be seen. Some men of 8/KG 51
e engaged in refuelling the aircraft for the coming mission.

Above: For easy transportation, heavy payloads were packed
in large wooden containers. To save personnel these were
moved by POWs and Russian *Hiwis* (an abbreviation of
Hilfswillige, literally translated as voluntary auxiliaries) –
men who collaborated with the *Wehrmacht* in Russia.
Thousands of these volunteers, a few of whom are seen
here, assisted with the transportation of supplies and built
new airfields in Russia with captured materials.

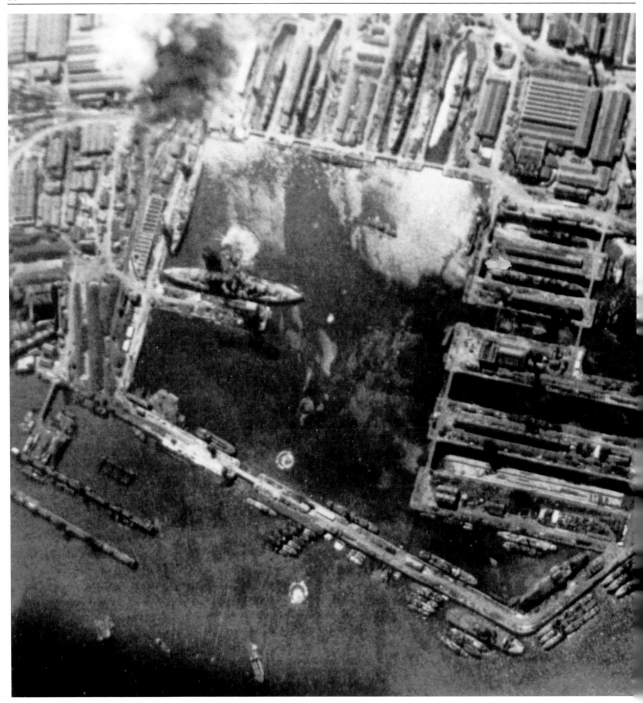

Above: During all sorties, photos were taken to identify the targets and to determine the level of success achieved on the mission. When attacking the naval harbour at Kronstadt this shot was taken by *Oberleutnant* Häberlen's *Beobachter* (observer or navigator) and shows a near miss by the battleship centre left. Other bombs have exploded in the supply stores nearby. Many small warships can be seen in different docks. Besides a cruiser, several destroyers, torpedo boats and submarines are visible. Two more water hits can be seen, left of centre, below the battleship.

Opposite page, top: This unarmed Ju 88A-4 was flown to KG 54 to become B+DF. From the 'black men' looking under

the wings, it is possible that a technical fault was found during one of the short inspections before take-off. The four-seater aircraft was painted in 70/71 and 65 colours.

Opposite page, bottom: The third *Staffel* of I/KG 54 'Totenkopf' ('Death's Head') was engaged in offensive operations in Russia in June 1941. This Ju 88A-5 has been given a black colour scheme for night operations. The *Balkenkreuze*, the standard crosses applied to the fuselage and wings, and the swastikas carried on the tail have all been painted over. In southern Russia the unit came under the command of the V *Fliegerkorps* which was part of *Luftflotte* Later the unit was reassigned to the Mediterranean.

Left: This Ju 88 A-4, B+CH, is operated by 1/KG 54 'Totenkopf'. Because there was a shortage of hangars, most repairs were carried out by civilian ground crew in the open, as seen here. Technicians from *Deutsche Lufthansa* together with specialists from the main aircraft manufacturers were needed to carry out many maintenance duties because of a shortage of military personnel. The fairings of the right engine have been removed together with the propeller. The lowered dive brakes can be seen under the right wing.

Opposite page, bottom: This Ju 88A-5 was shot down over the Soviet Union. Due to the pressure of Allied fighters and bombers over Western Europe the *Luftwaffe* was forced to send more fighter units back to Germany to strengthen the protection of the *Reich*. Because the German aircraft industry was unable to produce enough single-seat fighters many bomber operations in Russia were carried out with insufficient protection.

Below: This Ju 88A-6 (again, the distinguishing fairings can be seen) was operated by II *Gruppe* of KG 54 'Totenkopf'. The aircraft was shot down by Russian fighters. To prevent the destruction of the aircraft by German bombers the Russians have camouflaged it. It was later transported to an evaluation site.

Above: After an attack by a Soviet single-seat fighter this Ju 88A-5 of I/KG 51 was forced down and was damaged during the emergency landing in September 1941. The crew survived without serious injury. Although I *Gruppe* flew Ju 88A-5s (the A-5 preceded the A-4 model into operational use), these were equipped with A-4 type rear cockpit sections, which were bulged and had space for two rearward-firing machine-guns instead of just one. Despite this improvement they still suffered losses.

Below: This He 111H-3, 6N+HK, is part of 3/KGr 100 which carried out many pathfinder missions over England before it was sent to Russia in summer 1941. The tiny rod which can be seen projecting from the top of the wing, far left centre, is a visual indicator for the pilot (whose view of the wheels is obscured by the wing) that the undercarriage has lowered and locked into position.

Above: One of I/KG 27's He 111H-3 is prepared for an operation. The 'black men' are in the process of loading one of eight SC 250 bombs into the aircraft's vertical-slotted bomb-bay. Many of the bombers were loaded with two small incendiary bombs or a mixture of these and bombs fitted with the so-called *Jericho-Pfeifen* (Jericho Pipes) which produced a loud whistling as they descended.

Below: During the early years of World War II enough GP bombs were available to fulfil all the demands of the *Kampfgeschwader* and, during the first phase of the Russian campaign, the *Munas* (short for *Munitionsanstalten*, or Munitions Factories) which were responsible for filling the bombs with explosive loads could produce sufficient materials. In this picture, several SC 250B and five SC 500J bombs, of which two are equipped with the old fin section, await fusing and loading aboard bombers.

Oberleutnant Klaus Häberlen, who was later promoted to *Major*, became the commanding officer of I *Gruppe* of KG 51 between 5 February 1943 and 11 October 1943. During that time the '*Edelweiss*' *Geschwader* was commanded by *Major* Egbert von Frankenberg und Proschlitz and from 9 May 1943 by *Major* Hans Heise. On 20 June 1943 Klaus Häberlen, who seen here inspecting the results of enemy action, received the knight's cross.

above: After part of the main undercarriage broke away from this Ju 88A-4 of KG 51 'Edelweiss' on landing, the port wing and the elevator were damaged. The aircraft was immediately repaired by the *Feldwerftabteilung* (field workshop) which could repair nearly all damage caused in the daily operations of one of the *Kampfgruppen*.

right: This is a Croatian Volunteer crew (note the Ustachi emblem below the cockpit of the Do 17Z) operating with 7/KG 3 'Blitz' (aircraft code 5K + HR). The Do 17Z was later replaced with the Ju 88A-5.

Above: The number of warm-up systems, for heating up cold engines, were too few to make more than a limited number of *Luftwaffe* bombers available for daily operations during the Russian winter. One of the devices can be seen, on the right of the picture, being towed by an Opel *Blitz*. This ground crew wear fur coats and woollen caps. The aircraft they are attending has been given an improved defensive armament of two MG 15s in the nose.

Opposite page, top: During autumn and winter it was a hard for the ground crew to service their aircraft in the open. The number of hangars was limited due to the destruction caused by *Luftwaffe* attacks during the first few months of the campaign. This He 111H-4 of II/KG 55 which operated under the command of *Luftflotte* 4 over the southern part of the Russian Front is being cleaned by one of the 'black men' after the first snow of 1941.

Left: Here we see the Do 17Z, 5K+HR, of 7 *Staffel* of KG 3 '*Blitz*' again, this time manned by a German crew. Because of the poor performance of these twin-engined bombers they were withdrawn. The III *Gruppe* of KG 3 then received Ju 88A-5s which were themselves replaced by more powerful A-4s early in 1942.

Above: This He 111H-5 was flown by crews of 6 *Staffel* of KG 53. The unit was one of the very few *Luftwaffe* bomber units which were used for pathfinder missions. On the top of A1+MP's fuselage the large antenna of the Y-equipment can be seen. The frontal armament comprised an MG FF (20 mm cannon) in the A-position and an additional MG 15 above. Note that under the wings of this pathfinder aircraft two ETC 50s (small bomb racks) have been installed because the bomb-bay has been fitted with auxiliary fuel tanks.

Opposite page, top: This photo was taken by a member of the crew of 5/KG 55 'Griffin' after an emergency landing. The He 111H-16 was armed with an MG 131 (13 mm machine-gun) installed in the armoured B-position (dorsal gun position). A fixed MG 17 (7.9 mm machine-gun) was installed in the extreme tail to increase the defensive capability of the twin-engined bomber when attacked from behind. Armoured glass gave better protection to the B-position gunner.

Right: This aircraft, 4D+CH, is part of 1/KG 30 '*Adler*' (eagle), identified by the unit's badge painted on the nose. The aircraft has just been refuelled from a *Betriebsstoffkesselwagen* (fuel servicing truck). Despite the winter conditions the aircraft still has 70/71 painted on the upper surfaces. Both dorsal positions have been improved by the installation of armoured glass. In the lower C-stand (ventral gun position) one MG 81 I or MG 81 Z (7.9 mm machine guns; the latter contained twin guns side-by-side: Z stands for *Zwilling*, or twin) was installed instead of a movable MG 15 machine gun.

Above: From time to time *Schleppgruppen* (glider-towing formations) and *Transportgruppen* equipped with He 111Hs were used to strengthen the offensive capability of the front line bomber forces over the Eastern Front. This He 111H-4 belongs to *Schleppgruppe* 4 and was photographed during winter 1943/44. It is protected by tarpaulins against snow which fell during the night.

Below: This He 111H-6 is one of the standard bombers used for offensive operations over the Eastern Front. This aircraft 1G+BH, part of 1/KG 27, is well camouflaged for winter. Because no hangar was available the aircraft was serviced outside, which meant that a lot of extra time and effort was needed to warm up the engines each morning.

bove: Containers like those illustrated here were used by everal *Kampfgruppen* and the *Transportgruppen* to drop upplies to besieged units of the *Wehrmacht.* The aircraft nown here belongs to *Transportgruppe* 30 and carries the actical code S3+. Many of the aircraft were given extensive inter camouflage and had no markings other than the *alkenkreuze* on the rear fuselage and upper wing surfaces. his one has a swastika on the tail. Undersurfaces were sually painted black.

Below: In the spring, the Russian airfields became very muddy and moving the aircraft was often impossible without the help of heavy trucks. This Ju 88A-4, 5J+FH, standing on an airfield on the Eastern Front, has just been warmed-up. It belongs to 1 *Staffel* of KG 1 'Hindenburg' which was part of *Luftflotte* 4. Barrels of fuel have been placed next to the aircraft ready for refuelling.

Above: There are several Ju 88A-5s of I/KG 51 *'Edelweiss'* on this airfield.
The nearest one, 1K+DL, is undergoing maintenance. Some of the crews
and most of the ground crew were often housed in camouflaged tents as
shown here. The few houses in the area were taken from their owners to
allow the aircrew better living conditions. To prevent destruction of the
aircraft by Russian fighter-bombers the bombers have been widely
dispersed around the airfield.

Opposite page, top: This Ju 88A-5 of KG 54 *'Totenkopf'* is being refuelled
for the next operation. The pilot stands behind the tailplane, supervising
the 'black men' while another member of the crew checks the engine's
nacelles. One MG 15 is installed in the aircraft's A-position.

Right: One of the crews belonging to I *Gruppe* of KG 51 posing in front of
their Ju 88A-5 after a successful return from a dangerous mission over
the central sector of the Eastern Front. The crew wear the typical summer
flying suits and blue *Luftwaffe* field caps. The rank insignia on their arms
indicate an *Oberleutnant* on the left and a *Feldwebel*, second from right,
displaying three wings on the sleeve of his jacket, and an *Unteroffizier* on
the far right of the shot.

A village of camouflaged tents for the ground crew of KG 51. The bomb-shaped object to the left of the shot is an airborne supply container used to transport essential equipment when units moved from one base to another. The crews took their *Ersten Wart* (leading mechanic) with them to their new base so that operations could be continued without interruption. Not the geese, possibly destined for the dinner table.

Right: This crashed Ju 88D-1, F6+AK, of 2(F)/*Aufklärungs-gruppe* 122 is guarded by a militiaman armed with an old rifle. During an emergency landing the fuselage of this long-range reconnaissance aircraft, painted in standard colours (70/71 and 65), suffered heavy damage to the fuselage and both wings. It was shot down by the Red Army.

Right: The cockpit of the same F6+AK being examined by Red Army soldiers. During the crash the cockpit section was destroyed. The wireless equipment can be made out at the rear of the cabin. Not much as remained intact.

Above: Long-range reconnaissance units were essential to a successful air war. This Ju 88D-1 of 2(F)/*Aufklärungsgruppe* 22, coded 4N+, was engaged in operations over the northern part of the Eastern Front. It seems that the crew is celebrating the completion of a large number of missions. The pilot is on the left and behind him is an NCO with the rank of *Oberfeldwebel*. On the right is a *Feldwebel* wearing a peaked cap (*Luftwaffen Schirmmütze*).

Below: This He 111H-4 is part of I/KG 4. It crashed after returning from a mission. It was one of a limited number of pathfinders equipped with an X-system (radio navigation system) for target location. Shortly before crash-landing the crew opened the glass fairings of the cockpit and the B-stand (dorsal gun position) so that they could exit the aircraft as fast as possible.

Above: The pilots, all officers of I/*Kampfgeschwader* 51 *Edelweiss'*, using bomb crates as a dining table. During the summer, flying personnel often took their lunch near their aircraft (in the background). The officers are wearing the standard blue field uniforms of the *Luftwaffe*. *Oberleutnant* Klaus Häberlen is second from right. He seems to be pondering the quality of the meal.

Below: The SC and SD 1400, 1700, 1800 and 2000 bombs were among the heaviest used by the *Luftwaffe*. Because only a limited number of these were available, only very skilled crews had the opportunity to drop them. The large bomb shown here is waiting to be loaded under one of the He 111H-20s of *Kampfgruppe* 100. The SC 2000 'Max' was 3.5 m in length and had a diameter of 0.66 m. It was filled with 1200 kg of explosive and destroyed everything within 100 m of impact.

Right: This Ju 88A-4 (or possibly an A-14) belongs to I *Gruppe* of KG 3 *'Blitz'*. The aircraft is being cleared of snow after an overnight snowfall. In the rear part of the opened entrance beneath the nose is a MG 81 Z which was intended to protect the aircraft against enemy fighters attacking from behind and below. Both rear cockpit positions (dorsal) have been armoured with thick glass to protect the gunners.

Left: Summer 1943. This Ju 88A-14 is being prepared for a night mission. Note that nearly all the undersurfaces have been painted black. Flame dampers (shrouds covering the exhaust stubs) were later introduced to aid concealment. The aircraft shown here belongs to II *Gruppe* of KG 6 which was commanded by *Hauptmann* Hans Mader who was later promoted to *Major*. He took command of I *Gruppe* in 1943.

Opposite page: An He 111H-6 of II/KG 54 carrying a huge SC 1800 bomb to a target in winter 1942/43. The well-camouflaged aircraft is fitted with one MG FF in the nose. The object on top of the cockpit is a rear-view mirror, indicating that the aircraft may have been used for towing supply gliders as the mirror helped the pilot to control the glider. Note the exhaust on the side of the Jumo 211D engine.

Left: KG 27 belonged to a number of *Kampfgeschwader* which were used mainly for supply missions. But this He 111H-5, or H-6, of II *Gruppe* is loaded with SC 250 bombs for a raid against enemy supply lines. The aircraft is armed with two MG FFs for low-level attacks, one of them being housed in the bulge under the fuselage. A servicing trolley in front of the aircraft helps to replenish the oil in both engines.

Opposite page, bottom: This He111 H-6 was operated by crews of II/KG 53 'Legion Condor' (A1+) and crashed after a transport operation. Together with H-6s, several H-11s, H-14s, H-16s and H-20s were used to transport a large number of supply containers to the units of the *Heer* which were being encircled by strong Soviet forces after the loss of Stalingrad early in February 1943. Many of the aircraft lost were subsequently destroyed by German personnel to prevent them falling into Soviet hands.

Below: The heavy snowfalls demanded the use of powerful snow-blowers, like the one shown here, to remove the snow from runways and perimeter tracks. Additionally, snowploughs, many civilian workers and all available soldiers were needed to clear away enough snow to enable the aircraft to take off in the morning. Light, medium and heavy snowploughs were fitted on all common trucks of the *Wehrmacht* to carry out this important duty.

Above: The small tree in the foreground is one of many that were used as runway markers and to mark perimeter tracks on snow-covered airfields. This He 111H-6 belonging to I *Gruppe* of KG 27 is ready for take-off. Note the worn camouflage paint, an indication of it having taken part in several missions.

Opposite page, top: The Opel *Blitz* was a 3-tonne medium truck. The *Blitz* chassis could be fitted with a variety of bodies according to the purpose to which the vehicle was to be put, such as a transport lorry or a medium fuel servicing truck. The *Blitz* shown here has an *Einheitsführerhaus*

(standard cab) the design of which allowed it be fitted to most truck models. The *Blitz* was the standard fuel servicing truck throughout the war.

Opposite page, bottom: An He 111H-6 during its warm-up. This aircraft, 5J+GM, belongs to 5 *Staffel* of KG 4 and is well camouflaged for winter missions. On a single bomb rack under the fuselage there is one SD 500 armour-piercing demolition bomb. Despite the weather the crews of KG 4 and the other operational units carried out several attacks on enemy supply lines to reduce the pressure on German ground forces during the winter of 1943/44.

Four or eight supply containers, each equipped with its own parachute, could be carried inside an He 111H-6 and similarly equipped versions of the medium bomber. Under the main fuselage of the H-11 it was possible to fix up to five large supply containers in addition to smaller ones. A cushioning buffer (known as a 'damper') was fixed to the bottom of each container to prevent damage to its contents when it landed.

Above: A close-up view of an He 111H-16 with two forward-ring MG FF cannon: one in the nose, the other in the ventral position (to the immediate left of the bomb's tail ring). The bomb is being carried on the port bomb rack. Aircraft like this were used to attack important railway targets and on low-level raids against moving trains far behind the front line. Note the bombsight in the front section of the glasshouse and the broad exhaust streaks on the undersurfaces of the wings.

Below: Some crews were forced to try emergency landings in the white wastelands after their aircraft were attacked by Russian fighters. This heavily damaged He 111H-6 was found by Finnish soldiers who saved the uninjured crew. Note the additional armour-plate which gave the dorsal gunner a little more protection when defending his aircraft against fighters attacking from behind.

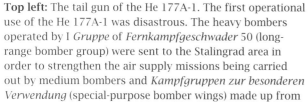

Top left: The tail gun of the He 177A-1. The first operational use of the He 177A-1 was disastrous. The heavy bombers operated by I *Gruppe* of *Fernkampfgeschwader* 50 (long-range bomber group) were sent to the Stalingrad area in order to strengthen the air supply missions being carried out by medium bombers and *Kampfgruppen zur besonderen Verwendung* (special-purpose bomber wings) made up from Ju 52/3m transports from flying schools and different transport formations.

Bottom left: A Hungarian Ju 88A-4 being loaded with an SC 500 GP bomb by ground crew trained by German specialists. Altogether Hungary received fifty-one Ju 88A-4s a few C-6 heavy fighters and some D-1 long-range

econnaissance aircraft. During the summer of 1942 the Hungarians carried out several successful raids but suffered heavy losses due to the lack of escort fighters.

Above: This Romanian He 111H-6 was one of ten aircraft handed over to V *Gruppe* between January and March 1943 and used on bombing raids. The remaining aircraft were later withdrawn for refitting following the arrival of *Luftwaffe* Ju 88A-4s. Some transport missions were also undertaken by Romanian crews to supply front line ground troops of Army Group South.

Above: This He 111H-6, 1A+DN, was flown over Russia by 5/KG 53
'Legion Condor' during winter 1942/43. After the unit took part in the
Battle of Stalingrad, II *Gruppe* was withdrawn to Kirovograd, Stalino and
Dniepropetovsk from where several targets between the Don and Donets
Rivers were attacked in February 1943 under the command of *Luftflotte* 4.
Many raids were made on important railway lines and crossings.

Opposite page, top: This He 111H-16 was operated by 8/KG 53 and was
among those aircraft that stayed in action until the end of 1944. The III
Gruppe, commanded by *Major* Emil Allmendinger between 24 June 1943
and 18 March 1945, was one of the units which mounted close-formation
attacks over Russia and over the sea. A part of the yellow band around
the rear fuselage has been painted black to prevent it from being seen
from the ground. All undersurfaces of the aircraft have also been painted
black.

Right: The I *Gruppe* of *Kampfgeschwader* 4, '*General* Wever', named after
the first Chief of Staff of the *Luftwaffe* (*Oberkommando der Luftwaffe*, or
OKL) who died in an air accident in 1936, was involved in many supply
missions between 1943 and 1945. The aircraft shown here, 5J+GK, is an
He 111H-16, recognisable by the well-armoured B-position. It is heading
for home after releasing its bombs. In the gondola under the fuselage
there are two MG 131s, instead of MG 15s or the single MG FF, to increase
its defensive firepower.

Left: This aircraft, A1+AC, belongs to the *Gruppenstab* of II/KG 53. The dorsal gunner of the He 111H-11 has opened his position to get a taste of fresh air in his compartment. A small mirror was fitted to the top of the cockpit to give the pilot a view to the rear. It was possible to load bombs up to 2000 kg externally beneath the fuselage and up to eight 250 kg bombs internally if no external bomb racks were fitted.

Opposite page, bottom: Crews of I/KG 51 standing in front of one of their Ju 88A-4s which were equipped with a bomb rack under the outer wings of the bomber. Two of the crew wear kapok-filled life jackets which, while they were fairly new could keep a man afloat for some 24 hours. The inflatable life jackets normally worn by fighter pilots and *Zerstörer* crews were better.

Below: There were four main sorts of aerial mine used by the *Luftwaffe*. The *Luftmine* A (LMA) and *Luftmine* B (LMB), which weighed 500 kg and 1000 kg respectively, were first dropped in British coastal waters in November 1939, and used intentionally over land during the Blitz of September 1940. The *Luftmine* C belonged to a smaller category and weighed some 600 kg. The *Luftmine* B shown here has fuses in the nose section as well as further back along the body.

Opposite page, top: Fitted beneath this He 111H-6 of KG 4 is a huge 700 kg supply container. Another one is in the foreground. There is a strong cushioning buffer installed at the base of the wooden canister. At the other end is a large parachute. The He 111H-6 shown here is well camouflaged over its upper surfaces with sand-coloured patterns.

Opposite page, bottom: Having flown their 300th mission this crew of *Kampfgeschwader 'Edelweiss'* pose in front of their Ju 88A-14 with its 20 mm MG FF in the gondola under the nose. The weapon has a flash suppresser to avoid giving away the aircraft's position when attacking a target. In June

and July 1943 the I/KG 51 used between two and five Ju 88A-14 bombers; its other bombers were the standard A-4 version, equipped with a bombsight in the gondola.

Above: The aircraft in the background is a Ju 88A-4, coded V4+, and belongs to KG 1 'Hindenburg'. A member of the ground crew helps one of the aircrew don his blue *Luftwaffe* overall (summer-weight flying uniform) under which he wears a pneumatic life jacket. Once inside his overall, the airman got into his *Luftwaffe* aircrew parachute harness. He wears the standard *Luftwaffe* cap, known as the *Schiffchen* (little ship) by the crews.

Above: After returning from a mission, a tired but unhurt crewman is brought by a *Gefreiter* to a waiting car. The aircraft, a Ju 88A-14, is part of *Kampfgeschwader 'Edelweiss'* and has returned intact. The officer on the left wears the summer-weight flying uniform and has the rank of *Oberleutnant* (equivalent to Flying Officer) and is part of the wireless section of I *Gruppe* of the *Geschwader*. Other officers standing around wait for news of the mission from the crew who have just returned.

Below: In the middle of 1944, the staff of *Kampfgeschwader* 1 'Hindenburg' together with its I and II *Gruppen* received the brand new He 177A-3, a heavy and powerfully armed two-engined bomber. Several of these were lost after the OKL sent a desperate order to fly low-level attacks against enemy tanks. Between 20 and 28 June 1944 a number of these missions were carried out. The remains of the *Geschwader* were withdrawn and sent to central Germany to be re-equipped.

Above: One of 1/KG 1's He 177A-3s which crashed after being severely hit by anti-aircraft fire while attacking Russian tanks on the battlefield. The well-camouflaged aircraft was severely damaged in the emergency landing and was later blown up by German troops. It is possible that they managed to dismantle both DB 610 engines (made by Daimler-Benz) for later installation in another aircraft.

Below. Another wreck of a twin engined bomber which had been destroyed by Allied fighter-bombers. After the explosion of the fuel tanks in the main part of the fuselage, the aircraft immediately caught fire. In the background, a Ju 188D long-range reconnaissance aircraft is taking off from its base in Poland for a mission over the Eastern Front.

Above: This group of *Luftwaffe* technicians and Russian *Hiwis* was responsible for recovering crashed *Luftwaffe* and enemy aircraft. Besides large trailers, the *Bergungs-kompanien* (recovery companies) were equipped with cranes and trucks to take damaged *Luftwaffe* aircraft to a *Feldwerftkompanie* (Field Workshop Company) for repair and to take crashed enemy aircraft to evaluation centres. On the lorry trailer behind this group, the fuselage of an He 111 awaits transportation.

Below: One of the He 111H-11s operated by 14 *Staffel* of KG 27 after a crash landing following enemy action. Some of these aircraft were used for low-level attacks against railway targets behind the front line. To avoid severe damage from barrage balloons cables, a so-called *Kutonase* (a horizontal metal strip which was looped around the nose just above the gun) was installed to cut the cables. An MG FF was installed in the nose for bombarding locomotives.

Above: This He 111H-20/R1 belongs to *Transportgruppe* 30 s part of its 1 *Staffel* and has a reduced defensive rmament. Only the movable MG 131 turret, the ventral 1G 81 I and the MG 131 in the gondola under the fuselage re fitted. Flame dampers have been fitted to the exhaust ystem. The aircraft is finished in a typical winter amouflage pattern.

Below: This aircraft, 5J+DC, is part of the *Gruppenstab* of II/KG 4 '*General* Wever' and flew several transport missions to besieged German units trying to defend their positions against the Red Army. During these missions the crews often attacked the enemy lines to support the encircled soldiers. The standard camouflage (70/71) of grey stripes has been sprayed all over the aircraft.

Left: The Ju 88S and T were operated in limited numbers over Russia. The Ju 88T-3 was fitted with two powerful Jumo 213A-1 engines and was flown by long-range reconnaissance units of the *Luftwaffe*. Most of these aircraft were fitted with flame dampers. Note the large wooden VS 11 propellers and the camouflage pattern on the upper surfaces while the under-surfaces are painted black. The picture was taken during a transfer flight to a front line unit in late 1944.

Left: The 3/KG 53 'Legion Condor' was equipped with the He 111H-11, illustrated here, which could carry all kinds of payloads. With a large multi-purpose bomb rack it was possible to carry up to three SC 1000 GP bombs, along with a large supply container or many smaller bombs packed into bomblet dispensers. Flame dampers have been fitted to the exhausts. Note the MG FF in the nose has been fitted with a flash suppresser.

bove: This He 111H-16, operated by an unknown unit, is ell equipped with FuG 200 radar, a cable-cutting system nd flame dampers. The aircraft may have been used as a ight intruder or for night transport flights far behind the nes. The photo was taken in autumn 1944 and shows a rew celebrating the completion of their 2000th mission. ote the placard.

Below: To prevent detection by enemy aircraft everything was done to camouflage bombers and transport aircraft on the ground. This He 111H-20, belonging to 9/KG 55, was used for supply flights to designated fortresses: ground forces besieged in towns by the advancing Red Army which were ordered by the Führer to hold out to the last man. But without the necessary weapons and supplies these fortresses could not hold out against an overwhelming enemy. Despite the camouflage nets the aircraft shown was not well concealed from the air.

Above: More and more Allied bombers and fighters destroyed the German infrastructure after 1943. This Ju 88A-4 was hit in October 1944 during a raid by fighters. Many German aircraft parked along the tracks heading to airbases became victims of fighters and fighter-bombers carrying out low-level attacks despite heavy concentrations of quad 20 mm AA guns. To assist the AA batteries all kinds of redundant machine-guns were removed from aircraft and employed as makeshift anti-aircraft weapons to defend airfields and other important sites.

Opposite page, top: This Ju 88S-3 was used as pathfinder for one of the last organised German operations over the Eastern Front. At the end of 1944 a few of these aircraft were equipped with up to four large 600-litre drop tanks to enable them to be used as pathfinders for *Misteln* (Mistletoes) which were to be sent to destroy important targets far behind the front line. The antennae of the FuG 216 rearward-looking warning radar can be seen on the wings.

Right: The Ju 88G-10 Mistletoe with a Fw 190F-8 fighter was chosen to carry out the operation '*Eisenhammer*' (iron hammer) planned for April 1945. Because the Red Army advanced faster than estimated the range of the Mistletoe was insufficient to reach its target. This Mistletoe was captured by American soldiers in central Germany.

Above: These Ju 188F-1 and D-1 aircraft belong to the long-range reconnaissance units of the *Luftwaffe* but also took part in the last offensive raids. Together with Do 217M-1s of the former *Aufklärungsgruppe Nacht*, the 4(F)/*Aufklärungsgruppe* 14 was used to fly armoured reconnaissance missions over the eastern battlefields. Besides propaganda leaflets, SD 70 bombs were dropped but only a limited success was achieved.

Below: By the end of World War II, the remaining German combat aircraft, such as this Ju 188, together with a Bf 109C and an Fw 190D-9, were constructed only to be scrapped within the following two years without ever entering comba